THE PALEO SLOW COOKER COOKBOOK

40 Easy To Prepare Paleo Recipes For Your Slow Cooker

Martha Drummond

i

Table of Contents

Introduction

Many paleo diet recipes you find require a lot of prep time, but you lead a busy life and you probably do not have time to spend hours in the kitchen. The good news is that following a paleo diet does not have to mean spending hours cooking healthy recipes. By using your slow cooker, you can put together healthy paleo meals without a lot of work. Simply add ingredients to your slow cooker, turn it on and then go to your job. You will come home to a delicious, paleo dinner that lets you relax in the evening instead of scrambling around to prepare a meal.

From breakfast dishes, to dinner recipes, to fabulously decadent desserts, you will find it all in this paleo slow cooker cookbook. It is packed with recipes that are all paleo, so you can stick to your healthy paleo diet while enjoying the ease and convenience of cooking with a slow cooker. While you are sure to appreciate all the amazing recipes included in this paleo slow cooker cookbook, you will also enjoy some helpful information on the paleo diet, the benefits of eating paleo and some slow cooker tips that will help you make sure that every recipe turns out wonderfully.

Chapter 1: The Paleo Diet, Paleo Benefits and Intro to Slow Cookers

Before you begin using the delicious paleo recipes included in this paleo slow cooker cookbook, it is important to take a closer look at the paleo diet, the benefits of this diet and the benefits of cooking paleo with your slow cooker. Whether you are new to the paleo diet or you've been following the diet for years, the information provided is sure to prove helpful as you continue along your paleo pathway. Here's a closer look at this popular diet, as well as some helpful information on using slow cookers.

About the Paleo Diet

Although the paleo diet became popular within the past few years, it is not a new diet. A book by Walter Voegtlin was published on the subject back in 1975, which brought the diet to light in the western world. Even after the book, the popularity of the diet didn't surge until after the beginning of the 21st century. The central concept of this diet is to copy the diet that humans ate during the Paleolithic Age, thousands of years ago. The diet of Paleolithic man was low in carbs and high in protein and Voegtlin claimed that this diet offers many benefits. The paleo diet is one of many low-carb diets that have become popular within the past decade. While this diet is widely known as the paleo diet, some refer to it as the hunter-gatherer diet, the Stone Age diet and the Caveman diet.

The entire paleo diet is focused on mimicking the diet of our ancient Paleolithic ancestors, which involves eliminating foods from our diet that did not enter the human diet until after the Paleolithic Age, such as legumes, grains and other foods that are products of agriculture. The diet focuses on eating foods that would have been available to humans during the Paleolithic Age, as well as foods that can be eaten in their natural state. The claim is that the body adapted to the foods that were eaten during the Paleolithic era and the body reacted optimally to those foods. However, as agricultural products were introduced, the body began to suffer and unfortunately, those foods do not offer the nutrition benefits that foods from the Paleolithic era have to offer.

Unlike many diets, the paleo diet is designed to be a lifestyle instead of a fad diet that is used to provide temporary, fast weight loss. Of course, while this diet is low-carb, such as the South Beach and Atkins diets, there is no need to count calories or carbs while on the paleo diet. By focusing on eating the right foods, the diet helps individuals increase energy by eating more protein and helps to reduce carb intake, resulting in improved longevity and health.

What Your Paleo Diet Should Include

PALEOLITHIC DIET

Natural Oils, Tree Nuts

Fruit, Berries

Vegetables

Meat, Seafood, Eggs

As you begin cooking paleo meals, it is important to know which foods your paleo diet should include. This way you can choose recipes that fit into the diet. While it can be difficult to exactly replicate the foods that were consumed during the Paleolithic period, this list of foods is fairly close, although substitutions are made in certain cases. The following foods are the foods recommended for individuals following the paleo diet.

- Eggs and Meats – Eggs and meats are probably the most important foods eaten while following the paleo diet, since these foods offer you protein. Of course, ideally you should choose meats and eggs that come from animals that eat an organic, natural diet to best copy the diet of those living in the Paleolithic era. For example, cattle should be grass fed, chickens should be free range and fish should be caught in the wild if at all possible. The protein from meats and eggs helps to keep you feeling full, helps support healthy bones and muscles and boosts immune function.

- Fruits and Veggies – Most fruits and veggies are allowed on the paleo diet, although peas and green beans are not allowed because they happen to be legumes. There is a bit of disagreement among proponents of this diet as to whether regular potatoes should be included in the diet. However, sweet potatoes are encouraged. When it comes to fruits, it's best to limit fruit juices and dried fruits, especially for those trying to lose weight or those trying to control glucose levels. Fruits and veggies are an important part of the paleo diet because they offer the body important minerals, antioxidants, phytonutrients and vitamins.

- Seeds and Nuts – Seeds and nuts are a part of the paleo diet. However, the amount of nuts eaten should be limited for those who want to lose weight. Keep in mind, since peanuts are legumes, they are not allowed on this diet. In many cases, nut milks like coconut and almond milk are used instead of dairy milk. Seeds and nuts include healthy fats, which are important to the body.

- Oils – Oils that come from plants, such as coconut oil, nut oils and olive oil are fine on this diet. Canola oil is recommended by some as well.

- Drinks – Of course, water is definitely encouraged, as is tea. Sweet drinks should be avoided on the diet, as should alcohol. There is debate as to whether you should drink coffee or not while following a paleo diet.

Foods to Avoid on the Paleo Diet

Now that you are aware of all the foods you should be eating on the paleo diet, it is important to know what foods to avoid while on the diet. Knowing what foods to avoid will help you as you prepare meals, helping you adapt other recipes to fit your new paleo lifestyle. Here is a look at the food categories that are generally forbidden while following the paleo diet.

- Grains – Agriculture had yet to be developed during the Paleolithic era, so few grains were ever eaten. Grains, including corn and wheat products, should not be eaten on the paleo diet.

- Refined Sugars – Refined sugars are forbidden while on the paleo diet. However, pure maple syrup and honey are allowed in small amounts.

- Legumes – Legumes are discouraged while on the paleo diet, since most have to be cooked before they are eaten. This category includes peas, peanuts and beans.

- Dairy Products – During the Paleolithic period, animals were not typically domesticated, which means dairy products were probably not consumed. However, some feel that butter may be okay from time to time and if dairy products are eaten, raw forms should be used and the animals should be grass fed.

- Certain Oils – Certain oils should be avoided, such as corn oil, peanut oil, soybean oil, wheat germ oil, cottonseed oil and rice bran oil. Products containing these oils, such as mayonnaise, should also be avoided.

Paleo Diet Benefits

The benefits offered by the paleo diet are what make it so attractive to many individuals. As you begin cooking paleo slow cooker recipes, you will be ensuring that you and your family enjoy all these important benefits.

- Benefit #1 – Real Food Without Toxins – One of the main benefits of eating paleo is the benefit of eating real foods that do not include toxins. Processed, packaged foods are full of additives, preservatives, artificial flavorings and artificial colorings. This increases the intake of toxins, which can cause negative health issues to occur. As you eat real foods, you will not have to worry about consuming toxins and unhealthy food additives.

- Benefit #2 – Increase Nutrient Intake – The paleo diet also helps you to increase your nutrient intake. Instead of eating processed carbs that contain few nutrients, you will be eating berries, veggies, nuts, fruit, seeds and healthy fats, which all contain important vitamins and minerals.

- Benefit #3 – Weight Loss and Maintenance – Many people go on the paleo diet to lose weight and the diet does help with weight loss for those that stick to the diet and engage in regular activity. Not only can it help you lose weight, but sticking with the paleo lifestyle can help you maintain that weight loss as well.

- Benefit #4 – Reduced Bloating and Digestive Problems – Another important benefit of this diet is its ability to reduce bloating and other digestive problems. The diet includes a lot of fiber, which helps to reduce problems with bloating, gas and other digestive issues.

- Benefit #5 – Stay Satisfied Longer – On the paleo diet, you will not be left going hungry. In fact, with the protein, healthy fats and fiber you eat regularly, you will feel satisfied longer than ever. While following the diet, you should not experience drops in energy, fatigue or the irritability that comes with drops in blood sugar.

- Benefit #6 – Increase Healthy Fat Intake – Many people today do not get the healthy fats they need, but the paleo diet is rich in healthy fats. These healthy fats help promote healthy skin, brain function and healthy arteries. Healthy fats also help to decrease inflammation throughout the body.

- Benefit #7 – Improve Control Over Blood Sugar – Studies have shown that the Paleo diet can help individuals with diabetes to improve control over their blood sugar, which is a significant benefit.

Of course, these are just a few of the important benefits that can be enjoyed when following the paleo diet. Other benefits that many people experience while on the diet include the following:

- Improved mental clarity
- Reduction in allergies
- Reduced pain from inflammation
- Better energy levels
- Improved immune function
- Better nutrient absorption
- Improved sleep
- Reduction in respiratory problems
- Increase in muscle tissue
- Improved mood
- Healthy hair and clear, healthy skin
- Lower risk of cancer, diabetes and heart disease

Benefits of Cooking Paleo Dishes with a Slow Cooker

For those who lead busy lifestyles, a slow cooker offers a variety of benefits. When you are very busy, it can be tough to make healthy, paleo meals. However, a slow cooker can make it much easier to put paleo meals on the table without needing to spend a lot of time working in the kitchen. Whether you are new to using a slow cooker or your slow cooker has a regular spot in your kitchen, it is important to consider all the benefits of using your slow cooker to cook delicious paleo dishes. The following are several of the top benefits you can enjoy when you use your slow cooker to prepare fabulous paleo diet recipes.

- Benefit #1 – Walk Away and Let Food Cook – When you use a slow cooker, you get the benefit of simply walking away and letting the food cook. You do not have to watch over the food as it cooks in the slow cooker. This allows you to throw ingredients in the slow cooker and walk away, taking care of other tasks or even heading to work while the slow cooker cooks your meal.

- Benefit #2 – Making Healthy Choices is Easy – When you are busy, it is tough to make healthy choices. You will find it easier to make the right choices and to stick with your paleo diet when you use your slow cooker. You can put together meals in advance and they will be ready when you are, so there is no need to make an unhealthy choice because you are in a hurry to get dinner on the table.

- Benefit #3 – Reduce The Time and Work Required to Cook Paleo Meals – Some paleo meals can require a lot of work, but when you use your slow cooker, you'll reduce the time and work required to cook up delicious, paleo meals. Paleo slow cooker recipes may require a bit of prep work, but most allow you to throw ingredients into the slow cooker and then you are done. You do not need to work for an hour in the kitchen to prepare the meal since the slow cooker does all the work.

- Benefit #4 – Stop Heating Up the Kitchen – Heating up the kitchen is a problem, especially in the summer. Instead of heating up your kitchen by using the oven, plug in your slow cooker and you can make tasty meals without heating up the kitchen and the rest of the house.

- Benefit #5 – Easy Cleanup – Easy cleanup is another benefit of cooking paleo dishes with your slow cooker. Many meals are completely cooked in the slow cooker, which means you only have to deal with cleaning a single pot after the meal, making cleanup a breeze.

- Benefit #6 – Save Energy – Using your slow cooker will even help you save energy. Since you are not using your electric oven or range, you will use less energy, since slow cookers use little energy. Saving energy means that you will also save money!

Slow Cooking Tips and Tricks

Slow cookers, often called crock pots, cook foods at low temperatures for 4-12 hours, in most cases. A consistent temperature is maintained by the slow cooker, which results in delicious, moist food. Since the slow cooker uses low temperatures to cook the food, it is possible to use long cooking times without worrying about burning foods. Slow cookers are perfect for cooking stews, soups, main dishes, desserts and sides, and it is easy to prepare foods the night before, then placing them in the heating unit to cook the next day. To help you enjoy all the benefits a slow cooker has to offer, here are a few slow cooking tips and tricks you will definitely want to remember for the best results.

Choose the Right Slow Cooker

First, it is very important that you choose the right slow cooker for your needs. For most of the recipes in this book, a round slow cooker will work perfectly. You will find that several different sizes are available when you are ready to purchase a slow cooker. For a family, four quart slow cookers work well for a family of four, while five or six quart slow cookers will work best for larger families. It is also important to ensure you choose a sturdy, high quality slow cooker that will provide you with delicious meals.

Avoid Overfilling the Slow Cooker

Another important slow cooking tip to remember is to avoid overfilling the slow cooker when you use it. It is usually best to avoid filling the slow cooker more than 2/3 of the way full, although this may vary depending on the brand of slow cooker that you purchase. If you overfill the slow cooker, it could make your meal take longer to cook and your food may not cook completely, causing a food safety hazard.

Remember to Keep the Lid On

When you cook with a slow cooker, it is tempting to open the lid to check out your cooking meal from time to time. However, it is important that you keep the lid on while the slow cooker is cooking. When you open the lid, it allows a lot of heat to escape from the cooker, which will make it take longer for your food to finish cooking. For every time you open the lid, it will require you to cook the food another 20 minutes to reach the desired doneness. The only times you should open up the lid is to check doneness when the meal is almost done.

Plan Ahead to Save Time

To save on time, plan those meals ahead of time. Just a bit of planning can save you a huge amount of time. For example, you can prepare ingredients for meals the night before so you simply need to toss them into the slow cooker the next morning to get your meal started. Just a little planning and preparation can go a long way when you are cooking with a slow cooker.

Consider Using Slow Cooker Liners

Another excellent tip to remember is to consider using slow cooker liners if you want to make slow cooking even more convenient. Slow cooker liners are plastic liners designed to withstand the heat of your slow cooker. All you have to do is place the liner in the slow cooker before you add the food. Then, when you are done with the meal, you simply throw the liner away and you do not have to worry about cleaning out the slow cooker. It makes cleanup a breeze and saves you a lot of time.

Know Low and High Setting Conversions

You also need to know the low and high setting conversions to make the most of your slow cooker. For example, if a slow cooker recipe tells you to cook the food for 3 hours on high, you may want to slow down the cooking so the recipe isn't ready until later. On the other hand, the recipe may require you to cook the recipe for 8 hours on low, and you may want to speed that time up. The rule of thumb is to add or subtract four hours if you want to change between the high and low settings. For example, if the recipe calls for 3 hours on high, add 4 hours if you want to cook it on low, making the time 7 hours. If the recipe requires you to cook the food for 10 hours on low and you want it done faster, subtract 4 hours to cook it on high, which means you'll need to cook the recipe for 6 hours on the high setting.

Don't Add Too Much Liquid

Last, make sure that you do not add too much liquid when you are cooking in the slow cooker. Since the lid is closed the entire time you are cooking in a slow cooker, there is little evaporation of liquids when compared to cooking in an oven or on the stovetop. You will notice that most recipes for a slow cooker will call for about half the liquid called for in a conventional recipe. Do not be tempted to add extra liquid or you may ruin the recipe.

Cooking with your slow cooker can be a lot of fun. With these helpful tips and tricks, you'll get the best results from these delicious slow cooker, paleo recipes.

Chapter 2: Paleo Slow Cooker Breakfast Recipes

Have you ever used your slow cooker to cook up a nice breakfast? Many people haven't. However, a slow cooker makes it easy to throw together something the night before and then wake up to a delicious, healthy paleo breakfast. This way you do not even have to worry about breakfast when you roll out of bed. From a tasty breakfast apple cobbler to the amazing egg and sweet potato breakfast pie, you are sure to enjoy these taste bud tempting, paleo slow cooker breakfast recipes.

❧Paleo Sweet Potato and Apple Slow Cooker Breakfast Spread❧

This sweet potato and apple breakfast spread is delicious and it is so easy to make. Not only does it go wonderfully with any paleo breads you make, but it tastes wonderful over baked apples, paleo apple pie or even the breakfast apple cobbler below. It is so tasty that it can double as a dessert recipe if you do not want to eat it for breakfast.

Ingredients:

- 3 sweet potatoes, washed, peeled and diced
- ½ teaspoon of ground cloves
- ¼ cup of ground cinnamon
- 5 apples, peeled, cored and diced
- 1 tablespoon of nutmeg
- 1 tablespoon of pure cocoa powder
- 1 tablespoon of ground ginger

How to Make It:

Start by peeling the sweet potatoes and apples after washing them. Remove the cores from the apples.

Dice the sweet potatoes and the apples and then add to the slow cooker.

Add the ground cloves, cinnamon, nutmeg, pure cocoa powder and ground ginger to the slow cooker.

Use a wooden spoon to stir well to make sure the spices cover all the pieces of apple and sweet potato.

Turn the slow cooker on low and allow to cook for 8 hours.

When done cooking, take an immersion blender and blend the mixture until you have a smooth, creamy spread. You can also pour the mixture into a blender and blend if you do not have an immersion blender.

Servings:

Makes 10-12 servings.

❧Paleo Egg and Sweet Potato Breakfast Pie Slow Cooker Recipe❧

This delicious egg and sweet potato breakfast pie is packed with healthy goodness. The sweet potatoes add fiber and plenty of nutrients, while you will enjoy plenty of protein from all the eggs used in this pie. Although there is no crust to this "pie," you can cut it just like pie slices for easy serving. The best part about this recipe is that it is super fast to make, allowing you to put breakfast in the night before so it is ready for you to enjoy in the morning.

Ingredients:

- 1lb of paleo friendly pork sausage
- 8 eggs, beaten
- 2 teaspoons of dried basil
- 1 sweet potato, shredded
- 1 yellow onion, finely chopped
- Pepper and salt to taste
- 1 tablespoon of garlic powder
- Add extra veggies you have on hand, ie. squash, peppers, carrots
- Coconut oil

How to Make It:

Using the coconut oil, grease the slow cooker before adding ingredients to ensure the eggs do not stick.

Using a food processor, use the shredding attachment to shred the sweet potato. If you do not have the attachment, you can use a grater to shred the sweet potato, but it takes a bit longer.

Place the sausage, beaten eggs, basil, shredded sweet potato, onion, salt, pepper, garlic powder and any extra veggies in the greased slow cooker.

Mix the ingredients well with a spoon until well combined.

Turn the slow cooker on low and allow to cook for 7-8 hours, ensuring that the sausage cooks all the way through.

When done cooking, slice into pie slices and serve while hot.

Servings:

Makes 4-6 servings.

❧Paleo Bacon and Blueberry Slow Cooker Breakfast Carnitas❧

This breakfast recipe offers a unique combination of pork, bacon and blueberries, which offers a wonderful flavor when it is done cooking. You will be surprised at how delicious the blueberries are with the meats, especially with all the spices added to the recipe. There is plenty of protein in this recipe from the bacon and pork roast, so you will be full and satisfied when you are done eating this breakfast.

Ingredients:

- ½ cup of real, pure apple juice (no sugar added)
- Pork shoulder roast (2-3 pounds)
- ¼ cup of real maple syrup
- 2 cups of fresh or frozen blueberries (if you use frozen, thaw them first before using)
- ¼ teaspoon of nutmeg
- 1 teaspoon of cinnamon
- Pinch of black pepper
- ½ teaspoon of dried sage
- 1 teaspoon of dried parsley
- Salt to taste
- Fresh parsley, chopped for garnishing
- 5 strips of bacon

How to Make It:

Start by putting the pork roast into the slow cooker.

Add the apple juice to the slow cooker.

Take the maple syrup and pour over the roast to create a nice glaze.

Sprinkle the roast with the salt, cinnamon, dried sage, pepper, nutmeg and dried parsley. Top the roast with the blueberries.

Turn the slow cooker on low and cover the roast. Allow to cook for 8 hours or overnight.

After the pork finishes cooking, remove the roast and shred the pork. To keep the pork moist and full of flavor, pour a bit of the liquid from the slow cooker over the shredded pork.

In a pan, cook the slices of bacon. Once bacon is done, remove half of the bacon grease, allowing half of the grease to stay in the pan. Allow bacon to cool on a plate covered with paper towels, then dice when the bacon is cool enough to handle.

Mix half of the bacon with the shredded pork, mixing well.

Place the pan back on medium high heat, allowing bacon fat to heat up.

Use a spoon and create patties out of the bacon and shredded pork mixture.

Place each patty in the skillet, pressing down and cooking on each side until crispy.

Place finished, crisp carnitas on a plate, top with a bit more bacon and then garnish with some of the fresh parsley.

Enjoy immediately.

NOTE: You could also cook up poached or fried eggs to put on top of the pork and blueberries.

Servings:

Makes 4-6 servings.

❧Paleo Chorizo and Egg Breakfast Slow Cooker Recipe❧

This breakfast casserole is extremely easy to make and you can easily put all the ingredients into the slow cooker and end up with a beautiful, delicious breakfast that requires almost no work on your part. After you try this recipe, you could also try the casserole with different combinations that you enjoy, such as kale and bacon or seasoned beef with mushrooms and spinach. You only have a little prep to do the night before, and then you let the slow cooker do the rest, allowing you to wake up to a cooked, tasty breakfast.

Ingredients:

- 12 eggs, beaten
- 1 lb of chorizo sausage, casings removed (check ingredients to ensure you have paleo friendly sausage)
- 1 small onion, chopped
- 1 butternut squash, small
- 1 cup of coconut milk

How to Make It:

Place the chorizo in a skillet and allow to start cooking.

After starting the chorizo, chop the onion.

After the fat begins rendering in the pan, add the onion and allow to cook until it becomes soft.

Take the chorizo and onion off the heat (sausage will finish cooking when it is in the slow cooker so no need to worry).

In a bowl, beat the eggs. Add the coconut milk and whisk until well combined.

Take the squash, peel it and remove all of the seeds. Then, chop the squash into pieces.

Use the coconut oil to grease the slow cooker to make sure the eggs do not stick and make a mess.

Add the onion and sausage mixture, the squash and the milk and egg mixture to the slow cooker. Stir together to make sure the egg mixture covers everything else in the slow cooker.

Turn the slow cooker on low and allow the casserole to cook for 8-10 hours overnight. When you wake it, it will be finished.

Serve and enjoy while the egg and chorizo casserole is hot.

Servings:

Makes 4 servings.

❧Paleo Maple Pork Breakfast Tacos Slow Cooker Recipe❧

Why not enjoy delicious tacos for breakfast? These maple pork breakfast tacos are sure to make your morning much better. They are full of flavor and the "tortillas" are full paleo and easy to make. Since this recipe takes a bit more work to make, you should save it for the weekend when you have more time. However, it does not take that long to prepare and the results are worth a little extra work. Your family is sure to love this delicious, protein packed breakfast.

Ingredients:

Tortillas

- ½ cup of coconut milk, canned
- Pinch of salt
- 2 tablespoons of coconut flour
- 3 eggs, beaten

Toppings

- 1 can of chopped green chilies (6-8oz)
- Green onions, chopped for topping
- 6 slices of bacon
- Hot sauce (paleo friendly), to taste

Shredded Maple Pork

- 2 teaspoons of garlic powder
- 2 lbs of boneless pork short ribs
- Salt to taste
- 2 tablespoons of maple syrup (more or less to taste)

How to Make It:

Add the pork short ribs to the slow cooker.

Top the ribs with maple syrup, salt and the garlic powder. There is no need for extra liquid due to the fat in the ribs.

Allow the ribs to cook for 8-10 hours or overnight.

The next morning, take ribs from the slow cooker and shred.

Place shredded pork in a bowl, topping with some of the liquid left over in the slow cooker. This keeps it from drying out and adds extra flavor.

To make the tortillas, whisk together the coconut milk, salt, coconut flour and eggs in a medium bowl. The mixture should be smooth.

Heat a non stick skillet on medium high. Place enough of the batter in the pan to make a tortilla, rolling the liquid around to make the tortilla as flat as possible. Cook for a minute on each side. Continue with the rest of the tortilla batter.

Meanwhile, add bacon to a skillet or to the oven, cooking until fully cooked. Chop bacon roughly after it cools enough to handle.

In a bowl, mix the hot sauce and green chilies, put in the microwave and cook for about two minutes.

To make the tacos, add shredded pork, bacon and green chili mixture to the tortillas.

Top with chopped green onions.

Eat right away and enjoy the delicious flavors.

Servings:

Makes 4 servings.

Paleo Breakfast Apple Cobbler Slow Cooker Recipe

This apple cobbler recipe is perfect for a sweet, delicious breakfast that will get your day started out the right way. The apples are spiced up with the addition of vanilla and cinnamon and the raisins and coconut add another layer of flavor to the breakfast dish. When you are ready to serve the dish, you can add some raw nuts and coconut on top to make it look wonderful as you serve it. It looks and tastes so wonderful that it makes a perfect brunch recipe when you want to impress guests.

Ingredients:

- 1 cup of raisins
- 12 apples, washed, cored and then chopped
- 2 teaspoons of salt
- 1 cup of shredded coconut
- 2 tablespoons of vanilla extract
- 1 cup of coconut milk
- 2 tablespoons of cinnamon

How to Make It:

Use a bit of coconut oil to grease the slow cooker.

In a large mixing bowl, combine the raisins, apple pieces, salt, coconut, vanilla, coconut milk and cinnamon. Mix together until everything is well combined. Pour the mixture right into your slow cooker.

Turn slow cooker on low and allow apple cobbler to cook for 6 hours or overnight.

When done cooking, serve immediately and enjoy.

You can top with extra shredded coconut and some raw nuts if desired.

Servings:

Makes 8 servings.

Chapter 3: Paleo Slow Cooker Snacks and Starters Recipes

You can even whip up some delicious paleo snacks and starters with your slow cooker. The best part about these snack and starter recipes is that you can put the recipe together, toss items in the slow cooker and then forget about it until it is done cooking. Whether you want to whip up a nice snack of honey cinnamon nuts or you want to cook some buffalo slow cooker hot wings to serve as starters for a party, you are sure to appreciate these easy, tasty recipes.

❧Paleo Jamaican Jerk Slow Cooker Chicken Wings❧

Instead of frying up wings, this tasty recipe allows you to skip the frying and make delicious wings in your slow cooker. They will be falling off the bone tender and juicy, and they are just as good as crispy wings. This recipe uses Jamaican Jerk seasoning for flavor, as well as apple cider vinegar, orange juice and lime juice. It offers a combination of flavors that will make your taste buds sing. These wings are perfect for a game day party or for a family night snack with the kids.

Ingredients:

- 3-4 lbs of drumsticks or chicken wings
- 2 tablespoons of Jamaican Jerk seasoning
- Salt, to taste
- 1 tablespoon of apple cider vinegar
- 1 small lime, juiced
- 1 tablespoon of coconut sap crystals (if desired)
- 1 large orange, juiced (1/4 cup of juice)
- 2 tablespoons of coconut aminos

How to Make It:

Start by placing your wings or drumsticks on a foil lined pan. Sprinkle with a bit of salt and then place under the broiler in the oven. Allow to brown, broiling for about 4-6 minutes on both sides.

After the wings are browned, coat with the Jamaican Jerk seasoning, ensuring they are coated evenly.

In a small bowl, mix the rest of the ingredients together to make the marinade.

Place all the chicken in a large ziplock bag. Pour the marinade into the bag and close the bag. Shake to coat the chicken with the marinade. Place the bag in the refrigerator and allow to marinate overnight.

The next day, place wings and the marinade in the slow cooker. Turn the slow cooker on low and allow wings to cook for four hours.

Serve wings while hot and enjoy.

Servings:

Makes 8 servings.

❧Paleo Honey Cinnamon Nuts Slow Cooker Recipe❧

These honey cinnamon nuts are a tasty, nutritious snack that everyone is sure to enjoy. Not only are these nuts a healthy snack, but they are so easy to make as well. When you want a sweet treat from time to time, these nuts offer you a guilt free way to indulge. The nuts include healthy fats and they make the perfect crunchy snack, since they are a lot healthier than party snacks or chips. You are sure to appreciate the combination of sweet and salty, so get the slow cooker on and whip up a delicious batch of these nuts to satisfy your sweet and salty craving.

Ingredients:

- 1/3 cup of raw honey
- 1 cup of raw walnuts
- 1 cup of raw pecans
- 1 cup of raw almonds
- 1 ½ teaspoons of cinnamon

How to Make It:

In a medium bowl, mix together the almonds, walnuts and pecans. Add the cinnamon and mix.

Drizzle the honey into the bowl of nuts, tossing well to make sure that the nuts are completely coated with the honey and cinnamon.

Place the nuts in the slow cooker. Cover and set the slow cooker on low.

Allow nuts to cook for 1.5 hours in the slow cooker.

Remove nuts from the slow cooker and spread on a cookie sheet to allow them to cool.

Once they are cool, place in an airtight container and store at room temperature.

Enjoy whenever you have a craving for a sweet and salty snack.

Servings:

Makes 12 ¼ cup servings.

❧Paleo Buffalo Slow Cooker Hot Wings❧

If you have a craving for good, old-fashioned, buffalo style wings, this is the perfect recipe for you. It is adapted to fit the paleo diet and it does not lack in flavor at all. The bold flavors make it a wonderful snack or starter. Serve it up as an appetizer at your next party or make a batch to enjoy when you are craving a hot and spicy snack. Instead of wings, you can always use drumsticks if you prefer.

Ingredients:

-   3-4 lbs of drumsticks or chicken wings
-   4 oz of ghee, coconut oil or grass fed butter
-   ½ cup of paleo hot sauce, plus ¼ cup

How to Make It:

Start by browning all the chicken under the broiler in the oven, broiling on both sides until the chicken begins to brown and get lightly crispy.

Melt the oil, ghee or butter and place in a small bowl.

Add ½ cup of the paleo hot sauce to the oil/ghee/butter and mix together well.

Place chicken in the slow cooker.

Pour the hot sauce mixture over the chicken pieces.

Use a spoon to toss, making sure all the chicken is evenly coated with the sauce. Top with the ¼ cup of hot sauce.

Cover the slow cooker and turn the slow cooker on low. Allow chicken to cook for 4 hours.

Serve while hot with extra paleo hot sauce as desired.

Note: For extra flavor, you can allow wings to marinate in hot sauce overnight before cooking in the slow cooker.

Servings:

Makes about 8 servings.

❧Paleo Honey Butter Roasted Walnuts Slow Cooker Recipe❧

If you have ever had roasted nuts at the fair or a carnival, you are sure to love this recipe. These nuts are even better and they taste amazing. When you make these in the slow cooker, your entire home will smell amazing and you will have a tough time waiting to sample these delicious nuts. Make them up and enjoy snacking on them when you want a tasty, sweet yet healthy treat.

Ingredients:

- ¼ cup of honey
- ½ teaspoon of pumpkin pie spice
- 3 tablespoons of grass fed butter
- 2 cups of raw walnuts
- 1 teaspoon of vanilla extract

How to Make It:

Place the grass fed butter directly in the slow cooker.

Turn the slow cooker on high and allow the heat to melt the butter.

After the butter melts, add the pumpkin pie spice, honey and vanilla to the butter, mixing together until ingredients are well combined.

Add the walnuts to the slow cooker and use a wooden spoon to toss the nuts until they are well coated with the butter and honey mixture.

Allow nuts to cook on high for 1-2 hours. You should check the walnuts from time to time, opening the lid and stirring them every half hour to ensure you do not burn the walnuts on the bottom of the slow cooker. Do not allow nuts to overcook.

Remove from slow cooker and enjoy. Leftovers can be stored in the refrigerator as long as they are placed in an airtight container.

Servings:

Makes 8 ¼ cup servings.

Chapter 4: Paleo Slow Cooker Main Dish Recipes

When you are looking for the perfect dinner recipe, these recipes are sure to please. Each recipe makes a delicious main dish that follows paleo guidelines while offering taste bud tempting flavor. Many recipes can be put together hours in advance and then slow cooked throughout the day, which allows you to have a nice dinner waiting for you at the end of a hectic day. The meatballs and spaghetti squash recipe is sure to be a kid pleaser and those who love Indian inspired food will appreciate the chicken tikka masala recipe.

❧Paleo Pineapple Chicken Slow Cooker Recipe❧

The combination of chicken and pineapple is simply delicious and you will end up with an amazing result when you try this tasty recipe. The chicken offers plenty of protein and the pineapple, clean salsa and zucchini offers plenty of nutrition. Your family will beg you to make this recipe again, so prepare to have no leftovers when you make it.

Ingredients:

- 2 jars (12oz each) of clean salsa
- ½ fresh pineapple, chopped
- 8 small zucchini, shredded
- 4 large skinless, boneless chicken breasts

How to Make It:

Start by washing all the zucchini, then use a food processer to shred the zucchini or use a grater to grate it.

Remove skin from pineapple and cut half of the pineapple into chunks for the recipe. Save the rest of the pineapple for a snack, breakfast or another recipe. Store pineapple and shredded zucchini in the refrigerator.

Place the chicken and the salsa in your slow cooker. Cover and cook on low for 4-6 hours or until chicken is very tender.

After the chicken is done cooking, use two forks to shred the chicken.

After shredding the chicken, mix the pineapple and the shredded zucchini into the shredded chicken.

Serve immediately and enjoy.

Servings:

Makes 8 servings.

❧Paleo Meatballs and Spaghetti Squash Slow Cooker Recipe❧

Spaghetti squash is the perfect paleo substitute for spaghetti noodles and this recipe makes it easy to make up meatballs and spaghetti squash for dinner. It is perfect for a day when you know you will be busy, since the food is ready to eat when it is done in the slow cooker. Just make sure that you find paleo friendly Italian sausage for the recipe to keep it to the paleo guidelines.

Ingredients:

- 1 lb of paleo friendly, ground Italian sausage
- 4-6 whole cloves of garlic
- 1 spaghetti squash
- 2 tablespoons of olive oil
- 2 teaspoons of Italian seasoning
- 1 14oz can of tomato sauce
- 2 tablespoons of hot pepper relish
- Parsley (for garnishing, if desired)

How to Make It:

Place the olive oil, hot pepper relish, tomato sauce, Italian seasoning and garlic in the slow cooker. Stir together until well combined.

Wash the spaghetti squash well and then cut it in half. Remove all of the seeds from the squash. Place the halves face down on top of the sauce in the slow cooker.

Take ground Italian sausage and roll into small meatballs. Place the meatballs around the spaghetti squash.

Cover the slow cooker and cook for about five hours on low.

Remove the spaghetti squash from the slow cooker, using a fork to pull out all the spaghetti from the squash.

Put spaghetti squash on plates and then serve with the sauce and the Italian sausage meatballs.

Garnish with a bit of parsley on the side if desired.

Enjoy while hot.

Servings:

Makes 4 servings.

❧Paleo Sweet and Spicy Slow Cooker Carnitas❧

Instead of going out for Mexican food, which can be hard to do when you are eating paleo, you can make these delicious sweet and spicy slow cooker carnitas at home, ensuring that all your ingredients meet your paleo diet. These carnitas are packed with flavor from the lime, tomatoes, onion and green chilies. You can serve up the carnitas in tasty lettuce bowls, topping with some guacamole and fresh, chopped tomatoes. You could even garnish with a bit of cilantro to add even more flavor.

Ingredients:

- 2 teaspoons of lime juice
- 2 tablespoons of orange juice
- 1 tablespoon of honey or agave
- 1 ½ cups of diced tomatoes
- ¼ cup of green chilies, diced
- 1 teaspoon of fresh garlic, minced
- ¼ cup of yellow onion, diced
- ½ cup of barbecue sauce
- ½ teaspoon of salt
- 1 tablespoon of cumin
- 1 teaspoon of garlic powder
- 2 teaspoons of chili powder
- 2 teaspoons of onion powder
- 2-3 pounds of pork shoulder or butt roast
- 4-6 lettuce bowls

How to Make It:

Place the pork roast in the slow cooker. Top with the chilies, onions, minced garlic and diced tomatoes.

In a small bowl, mix together the orange juice, lime juice and honey/agave. Combine until well mixed.

Add the cumin, chili powder, salt, onion powder, garlic powder and barbecue sauce to the juice mixture. Mix well.

Pour the juice mixture over the pork roast and veggies.

Cover and turn the slow cooker on low, cooking for 6-8 hours.

An hour before serving, use a fork to shred the pork, then stir all the ingredients together again to mix up the flavors. Allow to cook for another hour.

Serve the shredded pork carnitas in lettuce bowls. Top with guacamole, diced, fresh tomatoes, a bit of cilantro and any other toppings you desire.

Enjoy immediately.

Servings:

Makes 4-6 servings.

❧Paleo Lime, Cilantro and Chili Chicken Slow Cooker Recipe❧

You do not have to place a whole chicken in the oven to enjoy a delicious chicken for dinner. This recipe is made in the slow cooker and no one will ever guess that this chicken was not roasted in the oven. It is packed with flavor and comes out amazingly tender when it is done cooking. Allowing the chicken to marinate overnight in the marinade will make it even better. Even though marinating it takes a little extra time, you are sure to save time in the long run, since you can use the leftovers for other easy, paleo meals.

Ingredients:

-   ½ cup of fresh lime juice
-   1 tablespoon of olive oil
-   Dry rub (1 teaspoon each of pepper, sea salt and cumin and 1 tablespoon each of cayenne and chili powder)
-   2 handfuls of cilantro, fresh
-   3 garlic cloves
-   1 whole lime
-   1 large, organic, free range whole chicken (5-6 pounds)

How to Make It:

Take the chicken out of the packaging, rinsing it in cold water. Use paper towels to blot the chicken dry.

Using the dry rub you made, rub the chicken with some of the rub, making sure that the entire chicken is covered with the spice mixture.

In a food processor or blender, add the garlic, lime juice, olive oil and cilantro. Blend until you have a thick, even consistency.

Take the whole lime, using a fork or knife to poke many holes in it, and then insert it into the chicken cavity.

In a large crock pot liner or a large ziplock bag, place the chicken. Once the chicken is securely in the bag, pour the cilantro marinade over the chicken. Ensure that the chicken is coated evenly with marinade and use fingers to work the marinade under the skin. Use a knife to puncture the break area a few times so the marinade soaks into the meat. Seal the bag tightly and place the bag inside a pot or pan to make sure you don't have any leaks. Place in the refrigerator and allow it to marinate overnight.

The next morning, put the chicken into a slow cooker. Any leftover marinade should also go into the slow cooker.

Cover and cook on low for about 6-8 hours, or until chicken is fully cooked and tender.

Remove chicken from the slow cooker and serve while hot. Enjoy!

Servings:

Makes 6-8 servings.

❧Paleo Asian Inspired Pepper Steak Slow Cooker Recipe❧

This yummy pepper steak recipe is Asian inspired and is packed with Asian flavors that you are sure to enjoy. Cooking it in the slow cooker results in a tender, flavorful steak and veggies. When you want a different twist on steak, this recipe is one to try. The best part is that you can quickly throw this recipe together so you have a delicious meal ready for you at the end of the day with little work on your part.

Ingredients:

- ¼ cup of tamari (wheat free)
- 2 tablespoons of coconut oil
- 1 green bell pepper, cut into thin strips
- 2 cloves of garlic, minced
- 1 onion, cut into slices
- 1 can of diced tomatoes (16oz)
- 1 can of bean sprouts (16oz), drained
- 2 lbs of sirloin steak
- Pepper and salt to taste

How to Make It:

Place the steak on a chopping board, cutting it into ½ inch strips, cutting at an angle.

Heat the oil in a large frying pan.

Place the sliced steak into the pan, allowing to cook until it becomes lightly browned.

Drain away any fat and coat the steak with freshly ground black pepper.

Place the steak in the slow cooker.

Add the tamari and the minced garlic. Mix until the steak is coated with the garlic and tamari.

Cover the slow cooker and turn on low. Allow to cook for about 6 hours.

An hour before you want to serve the pepper steak, add the green peppers, onions, tomatoes and sprouts.

Turn crock pot on high and cook for another hour.

Serve while hot and eat immediately. Enjoy!

Servings:

Makes 4 servings.

❧Paleo Spicy Chipotle Beef Brisket Slow Cooker Recipe❧

This delicious beef brisket uses Chipotle adobo sauce for flavor, along with ground cloves, onion, oregano and apple cider vinegar. Once you make up the beef brisket, you can enjoy the meat wrapped in lettuce like tacos, you can serve it over salads for an easy, quick beef salad or you can even eat some leftovers with your eggs in the morning for a tasty breakfast. Enjoy having this brisket for dinner and then enjoy using the leftovers in different ways throughout the week.

Ingredients:

-   2 cups of beef stock
-   1 tablespoon of apple cider vinegar
-   ½-1 cup of Chipotle adobo sauce
-   3 cloves of fresh garlic
-   ½ teaspoon of ground cloves
-   2 bay leaves
-   1 white onion, chopped
-   2 teaspoons of oregano
-   1 beef brisket, 3-4 pounds

How to Make It:

In a food processor or a blender, combine the beef stock, apple cider vinegar, adobo sauce, garlic, ground cloves, onion and oregano. Process until you have a liquid puree.

Take about ¼ of the puree, placing it in the bottom of the slow cooker.

Add the bay leaves to the bottom of the slow cooker.

Trim excessive fat off the beef brisket, then place in the slow cooker, placing the fat side on the bottom. Leave only a little fat.

Take the rest of the puree, pouring over the beef brisket, ensuring that the sides and top are well coated.

Turn the slow cooker on low, cooking it for 8 hours.

When it is done cooking, remove the beef brisket from the slow cooker, using two forks to shred the brisket.

Place shredded meat in a bowl, then pour some of the leftover liquid from the slow cooker over the meat to ensure it stays nice and moist.

Serve the brisket in lettuce wraps, over a salad or in strips with vegetable side dishes.

Enjoy while warm.

Servings:

Makes 6-10 servings.

❧Paleo Chicken Tikka Masala Slow Cooker Recipe❧

This delicious Indian inspired recipe is packed with flavor. The coconut milk and garam masala add great flavors, as does the ginger, garlic, red chili flakes and the coconut palm sugar. The cilantro offers the perfect garnish that tops off this dish delightfully. Enjoy alone or you can serve it over cauliflower rice for a full meal.

Ingredients:

- 1 cup of coconut milk
- 3 cloves of garlic, minced
- 1 teaspoon of ground coriander
- 1 tablespoon of coconut palm sugar
- ½ teaspoon of salt
- 2 tablespoons of ghee or grass fed butter
- 1 tablespoon of ginger root, minced
- ½ yellow onion, sliced thinly
- 2-3 tablespoons of coconut oil
- 1 teaspoon of ground cumin
- ¼ teaspoon of red chili flakes
- 2 cups of crushed tomatoes, organic
- 1 tablespoon of garam masala, plus 2 teaspoons
- 2 pounds of chicken thighs, organic
- Fresh cilantro

How to Make It:

Remove any excess skin and fat from the chicken thighs.

Place thighs in a large bowl, sprinkling with a tablespoon of the garam masala, making sure the chicken is evenly coated.

Heat two tablespoons of the coconut oil in a skillet over medium high heat.

Place thighs in the pan, skin side down, allowing the thighs to sear.

Flip and sear on the other side. Seared thighs can be added to the slow cooker. Top with the sliced onion.

Melt the ghee or butter in a small sauce pan, add the garlic and ginger root, cooking until it sizzles.

Add the crushed tomatoes and the coconut milk.

Place the rest of the garam masala, cumin, red chili flakes, coconut palm sugar, coriander and salt in the butter mixture.

Allow to simmer until the spices mix together well and it begins to pop and simmer. Remove from heat, pouring the sauce over the chicken and onions.

Cover the slow cooker, turn on low heat and allow to cook for three hours.

Thighs should be fully cooked and the onions should be tender. If the chicken needs a bit more time, cook for another hour.

Serve while hot alone or over cauliflower rice, topped with a bit of chopped cilantro. Enjoy.

Servings:

Makes 5 servings.

❧Easy Paleo Pulled Pork❧

Pulled pork is a an extremely easy meal to make. It tastes great and it can be eaten in so many different ways. Enjoy warm, comforting pulled pork with some veggie sides, or add the pork to a nice salad for some extra protein. It even tastes great with eggs for a nice breakfast that is packed with plenty of protein to keep you full all day long. You are sure to enjoy the subtle seasonings in this recipe, including the chipotle powder, chili powder and cumin. Since the recipe goes in the slow cooker, you can get it ready, place it in your slow cooker and then walk away while dinner cooks. While you will need to do a bit of preparation to get it ready, once it is in the slow cooker, you can forget about it until it is done cooking, which makes for a no-fuss, easy dinner.

Ingredients:

- 2 yellow onions, thinly sliced
- 2 teaspoons of onion powder
- 3 tablespoons of chili powder
- ¼ teaspoon of chipotle powder
- 1 teaspoon of coriander
- 2 teaspoons of sea salt
- 1 tablespoon of parsley, dried
- 2 tablespoons of cumin
- Pork butt roast 4-5 pounds

How to Make It:

In a small bowl, mix together the onion powder, chili powder, chipotle powder, coriander, sea salt, parsley and cumin. Ensure the mixture is well combined. Then, rub the pork butt roast with this dry rub you have created, using all of it.

In the slow cooker, layer on half of the sliced yellow onions. Place the pork roast on top of the onions, then top with the rest of the yellow onions. Do not add liquid to the slow cooker.

Allow the roast to cook for about 5-6 hours on high. Reduce heat to low, then cook for another 3-4 hours. Roast should be falling apart done, making it easy for you to shred using a couple forks. Eat while warm and enjoy.

Servings:

Makes 10-14 servings.

Chapter 5: Paleo Slow Cooker Soups and Stews Recipes

Soups and stews are delicious during the cool winter months, but they make great lunches and dinners all year long too. This chapter is packed with some of the best paleo slow cooker soup and stew recipes, and these recipes are easy to put together in no time. If you are craving Mexican flavors, try the chicken enchilada slow cooker stew, or give the beef and garlic slow cooker stew a try when you need a quick, hearty, filling dinner.

❧Paleo Cinnamon and Apple Cider Butternut Squash Soup❧

This butternut squash soup is super easy to make and it is packed with veggie goodness. While the recipe calls for apple cider and cinnamon, you can always tweak the soup to meet your specific tastes, although the sweetness makes for a comforting bowl of soup. You'll get your servings of both fruits and veggies when you cook up this tasty soup recipe.

Ingredients:

- 2 cups of apple cider, no sugar added
- 1 teaspoon ground cinnamon
- 1 14oz can of coconut milk
- 1 medium carrot, washed, peeled and finely chopped
- 1 butternut squash, cut into cubes
- 1 teaspoon ground nutmeg
- 2 apples (any kind), washed, cored, peeled and diced

How to Make It:

Place the apple cider, cinnamon, coconut milk, carrot, squash, nutmeg and diced apples in a slow cooker.

Cover and cook on low for about 4-6 hours.

When soup is finished, use an immersion blender to puree the soup until it is smooth. You can also use a food processor or a blender if you do not have an immersion blender, but it should cook before you transfer the soup.

Serve up soup, garnishing with pumpkin seeds, bacon, cinnamon or nutmeg if desired.

Enjoy.

Servings:

Makes 8 servings.

❧Paleo Chicken, Kale and Cashew Slow Cooker Soup❧

If you are looking for a tasty, unique soup to try, you are sure to enjoy this fantastic soup. The cashews and cashew butter adds plenty of flavor to the soup, while the kale adds a chewy, hearty texture. Packed with delicious veggies, this soup is packed with nutrition. It is perfect for lunch or dinner.

Ingredients:

- 3 shallots, sliced thinly
- 1 can of fire-roasted, diced tomatoes
- ¼ teaspoon of cayenne pepper
- 1-2 tablespoons of coconut oil (or fat of choice)
- 1 bunch of kale, stems removed and torn into bite sized pieces
- 1 tablespoon of fresh ginger, grated
- 4-6 cups of chicken broth
- ½ cup of creamy cashew butter
- 2 chayote squashes, diced
- 1 tablespoon of minced garlic
- Pepper and salt to taste
- 1-2 ounces of crushed cashews for garnishing
- 8 ounces of boneless, skinless chicken breasts, cut into cubes

How to Make It:

In a skillet, heat up the coconut oil over medium high heat. Once the oil is hot, place the shallots in the pan, allowing to cook until they are crispy and brown.

Reduce heat to medium, adding the cayenne, garlic and ginger. Allow to cook for another minute.

Add pieces of chicken, cooking until it begins to color.

Place the chicken mixture in the slow cooker.

Add four cups of the chicken broth, pouring over the chicken.

Add the kale, chayote squash and tomatoes.

Cover the slow cooker and cook on low for about 6 hours or until veggies are tender and chicken is fully cooked. If needed, you can add more of the chicken broth.

About 30 minutes before serving, take out a bit of broth and mix it together in a bowl with the cashew butter.

Place back in the slow cooker, stirring to mix the butter throughout the soup.

Add a bit of salt and pepper to taste. Allow to cook for another 30 minutes.

Serve while hot, garnishing with some crushed cashews. Enjoy.

Servings:

Makes 4 servings.

❧Paleo Jambalaya Slow Cooker Recipe❧

If you like jambalaya, you will love this spicy, savory dish. Not only is it a comforting food to enjoy, but it is easy to make and will not require a lot of your time in the kitchen. All the spices are perfect for clearing your sinuses if you have a cold as well, but you can always adapt the recipe to be a bit less spicy if you desire. For the Andouille, make sure that it is hormone and nitrate free. When choosing the peppers for the jambalaya, it's nice to choose bell peppers in different colors, since it will add color to the jambalaya.

Ingredients:

- 1 large yellow onion, diced
- 1 lb of raw, de-veined, large shrimp (sustainably caught)
- ½ head of cauliflower
- 4 bell peppers, in any color, diced
- 2 cups of okra
- ¼ cup of paleo hot sauce
- 5 cups of free range chicken broth (or make your own)
- 2 cloves of garlic, minced
- 3 tablespoons of Cajun seasoning
- 2 bay leafs
- 4 ounces of diced chicken
- 1 can of diced tomatoes, organic, with the juice
- 1 package of paleo friendly Andouille sausage

How to Make It:

Start by placing the onions, chicken, hot sauce, tomatoes, peppers, garlic, bay leafs, okra and Cajun seasoning in the slow cooker.

Add the chicken broth to the pot. Mix everything together, cover, and then cook on low for about six hours.

About 45 minutes before serving, cut up the sausage and cook until almost done in a skillet. Add to the slow cooker when jambalaya is only 30 minutes away from being cooked.

Meanwhile, as the soup finishes, add the raw cauliflower to a food processor, processing until it is shredded to look like rice.

Add the shredded cauliflower and the raw shrimp to the soup for the last 20 minutes of cook time.

When the jambalaya is done, serve up in soup bowls while steaming hot.

Enjoy right away.

Servings:

Makes 4-8 servings.

⮞Paleo Chicken Enchilada Slow Cooker Stew⮜

If you enjoy all the flavors from enchiladas, you are sure to enjoy this chicken enchilada stew. It has all the flavor of enchiladas without worrying about what to wrap the enchiladas in, since you are not eating wheat or corn products. All the green chilies, tomatoes and jalapenos really add spiciness to the soup, and the chili powder and cumin add even more flavor to the mix.

Ingredients:

-   1 can of chopped green chilies, 4oz
-   3 cloves of garlic, minced
-   2 teaspoons of dried oregano
-   1 green pepper, diced
-   2 tablespoons of coconut oil
-   1 tablespoon of cumin
-   1 can of chopped jalapenos, 4 oz
-   1 tablespoon of chili powder
-   Pepper and salt to taste
-   1 can of tomato sauce, 7oz
-   1 can of diced tomatoes, 14oz
-   Avocado and cilantro for garnishing
-   2 lbs of boneless, skinless chicken breasts

How to Make It:

Place the chicken breasts in the slow cooker. Top with the rest of the ingredients except for the avocado and cilantro.

Cover and turn on low, allowing to cook for 8-10 hours of low.

Before serving, use a fork to shred up the chicken, stirring it up with the rest of the ingredients.

Serve into soup bowls, garnishing it with slices of avocado and chopped cilantro.

Eat while it's hot.

Servings:

Makes 4-6 servings.

Paleo Chicken and Lime Slow Cooker Soup

This chicken and lime slow cooker soup also takes inspiration from Mexican dishes, taking a classic comfort food to a whole new level with limes, garlic and chipotle chiles. Avocados add some healthy fats to the mix, and you will enjoy plenty of protein from the chicken in the soup. It is a perfect meal for lunch, but it is hearty enough to serve up for dinner as well.

Ingredients:

- 6 cloves of garlic, sliced thinly
- 2 limes, juiced
- 1 sweet onion, chopped finely
- 6 cups of free range or homemade chicken broth
- 1 avocado, sliced into 12 thin pieces
- ½ cup of fresh cilantro, chopped
- 2 tablespoons of olive oil
- Pepper and salt to taste
- 2 chipotle chilies from a can
- 2 tablespoons of the adobo sauce
- 6 boneless, skinless chicken thighs, cut into ½ inch chunks

How to Make It:

In a small skillet, heat up the olive oil on medium high heat, adding the garlic and onion to the pan.

Reduce heat to medium, cooking the onion and garlic for about 6-7 minutes.

Add the chicken to the pan, cooking until lightly browned, or for about 4-5 minutes.

Place the cooked garlic, chicken and onion in a slow cooker.

Stir in the chicken broth, the adobo sauce and the chipotles. Stir well until everything is thoroughly combined.

Cover and cook on low for 7-8 hours, or until chicken is fully cooked.

About 15 minutes before serving, add salt and pepper to taste. Then add the lime juice and sprinkle in the cilantro.

Cover and keep warm for the last 15 minutes.

In six soup bowls, add 2 slices of avocado.

Top with the soup. Garnish with more cilantro if desired.

Enjoy while warm.

Servings:

Makes 6 servings.

❧Paleo Thai Inspired Chicken Soup Slow Cooker Recipe❧

With a slow cooker, making the broth for your own delicious chicken soup is so simple. If you have ever had Thai chicken soup, then you are sure to love this Thai inspired slow cooker chicken soup. It is such a simple recipe, but packed with delicious, comforting flavors that your whole family will appreciate. Serve it for a simple lunch or before the main course at dinner.

Ingredients:

- 5 slices of ginger, fresh
- 1 tablespoon of salt
- 1 whole chicken
- 1 lime
- 20 basil leaves, fresh (save 10 leaves for garnish)
- 1 lemongrass stalk, cut into chunks
- More salt to taste if needed

How to Make It:

Add 10 of the basil leaves, the tablespoon of salt, chicken, ginger and lemongrass to your slow cooker.

Fill the slow cooker with enough water to cover the chicken.

Cover and turn the slow cooker on low.

Cook the soup for 8-10 hours.

Carefully remove the chicken and save to use the meat for another meal.

Ladle the chicken soup into bowls, adding a bit of fresh lime juice and salt to taste.

Garnish the bowls of soup with the remaining fresh basil leaves.

Servings:

Makes 10 1-cup servings.

Paleo Beef and Garlic Slow Cooker Stew

For a rainy day, this stew is a wonderful way to warm up. The recipe is easy to make and the stew is comforting and delicious. Not only does it include plenty of grass fed stew meat for protein, but the stew is packed with delicious veggies, not to mention all the healthy garlic the stew calls for as well. This soup is not only delicious, but it packs a powerful nutritious punch as well.

Ingredients:

- 6 medium carrots, peeled and diced
- 1 ½ teaspoons of ground marjoram
- 1 yellow onion, chopped
- 8-12 cloves of garlic, mashed or crushed
- 6 stalks of celery, chopped
- 1 small can of tomato paste
- Black pepper and sea salt to taste
- A splash of chicken broth
- 1.5-2 lbs of grass fed beef, cut as stew meat

How to Make It:

Place all the ingredients in the slow cooker. Use a spoon to mix them together.

Turn the slow cooker on low, cover and cook all day or about 8-10 hours.

As the stew cooks, the garlic will mellow out.

When the stew is done cooking, serve up in soup bowls and enjoy while warm.

Servings:

Makes 4-6 servings.

Chapter 6: Paleo Slow Cooker Side Dish Recipes

If you are using your oven for a main dish, consider using your slow cooker to make up a delicious side dish. This is perfect if you are serving a big dinner for friends and family or if you want to put together a side dish to take along with you to a potluck. Whatever the occasion, you are sure to enjoy these tasty, paleo side dishes. The bacon Dijon Brussels sprouts combine unique flavors for a great side, while the red cabbage side dish offers simple, delicious flavors that everyone will enjoy.

❧Paleo Red Cabbage Side Dish Slow Cooker Recipe❧

This side dish recipe uses red cabbage, along with an apple and raisins, which gives the dish a hint of sweetness. After cooking in the slow cooker, the flavors combine for a delicious side dish that will go wonderfully with a paleo main dish.

Ingredients:

- 1 red onion, chopped
- 2 bay leaves
- 1 head of red cabbage, chopped
- 1 cup of chicken broth
- ½ cup of raisins
- 1 gala apple, chopped
- Pepper and salt to taste

How to Make It:

Wash the head of cabbage and then remove the core.

Chop the cabbage into large pieces, which is fine since it will all cook down.

Wash the apple and the onion.

Chop the onion.

Core and peel the apple, chopping into bite sized pieces.

Add all the ingredients to the slow cooker. Use a spoon to stir the ingredients to combine.

Cover and turn on low, cooking for 4-5 hours.

When the cabbage is done cooking, stir once again before serving.

Serve and eat while hot.

Servings:

Makes 4 servings.

❧Paleo Sage Orange Sweet Potato Slow Cooker Recipe❧

If you love sweet potatoes, this side dish is for you. It makes a perfect addition to your meal on days that you work out, since healthy carbs are important when you work out. This side dish goes wonderfully with a simple chicken main dish as well. The orange juice, bacon and honey all combine with the sweet potatoes to create a delicious, lip-smacking dish!

Ingredients:

- 3 tablespoons of grass fed butter, cut into little pieces
- ¼ cup of orange juice (no sugar added)
- 1/8 teaspoon of salt
- 2 tablespoons of honey
- 1 teaspoon of sage
- ½ teaspoon of thyme
- 4 strips of cooked bacon, crumbled
- 3 large sweet potatoes, chopped into bite sized pieces

How to Make It:

Start by greasing the inside of the slow cooker using a bit of the butter, olive oil or some coconut oil.

Peel the sweet potatoes and then chop into bite sized pieces. Make sure pieces are nearly the same in size so they cook uniformly.

Add the sweet potatoes to the slow cooker.

In a small bowl, combine the orange juice, salt, honey, sage and thyme. Mix together well.

Pour the orange juice mixture over the sweet potatoes.

Take the small pieces of butter, placing on top of the potatoes so it will melt into the mixture as it cooks.

Cover and allow to cook for 2.5-3 hours on low heat.

Serve the potatoes while hot, topping with the crumbled bacon.

Servings:

Makes 4-6 servings.

Paleo Bacon Dijon Brussels Sprouts Slow Cooker Recipe

Brussels sprouts are so good for you and this recipe adds plenty of flavor to this veggie, making it a delicious side dish to serve up with nearly any meal. With the addition of the bacon, even the kids may end up liking Brussels sprouts after they try this recipe. The Dijon mustard adds an unexpected tang to the dish that really stands out when you try it. Since you can make this in the slow cooker, you will leave the stove or oven free for the main dish you decide to make for dinner.

Ingredients:

- 2 tablespoons of free range butter
- 1 lb of Brussels sprouts
- 6 oz of bacon ends, cooked until crisp
- 1 tablespoon of Dijon mustard
- Salt and pepper to taste

How to Make It:

In a frying pan, cook the bacon ends until they are nice and crisp. Allow them to cool and then cut or crumble into pieces.

Wash all of the Brussels sprouts, removing the ends from every one. Slice the Brussels sprouts in half and then add to the slow cooker.

Add the Dijon mustard, butter, bacon pieces, salt and pepper. Stir with a wooden spoon.

Add the lid and then turn the slow cooker on low, allowing the Brussels sprouts to cook for 4-5 hours.

Serve immediately and enjoy while warm.

Servings:

Makes 4 servings.

❧Paleo Slow Roasted Beets Slow Cooker Recipe❧

If you love eating beets from time to time, you are going to love this recipe. While the recipe is very basic, you can always spice up this side dish by adding some garlic or your favorite herbs to the slow cooker with the beets. However, this simple recipe really allows the flavor of the beets to shine through.

Ingredients:

- 1/3 cup of water
- 1 bunch of beets
- Salt, pepper and herbs to taste, if desired

How to Make It:

Wash the beets, then peel them and chop them into bite size pieces.

Place the beets in the slow cooker, adding any salt, pepper or herbs you want to add.

Pour the water over the beets.

Cover and turn the slow cooker on low, allowing to cook for 6 hours on low.

Serve beets while hot and enjoy.

NOTE: Before chopping beets, wear an apron to avoid staining clothes.

Servings:

Makes 2-4 servings.

Chapter 7: Paleo Slow Cooker Casserole Recipes

This chapter offers you some paleo slow cooker casserole recipes that allow you to make an entire meal in one pot. These casseroles are filling and you will not need to make anything else to go with the casserole. They are tasty and healthy too. The pizza bowl casserole is sure to be a hit with your kids and the sweet potato shepherd's pie casserole offers lots of nutrition in a one pot package.

❧Paleo Sweet Potato Shepherd's Pie Slow Cooker Casserole❧

When you need an easy meal that comes in a single pot, this is a great go-to recipe. It is made with healthy sweet potatoes and you can use your choice of meat, such as turkey, beef or lamb. The addition of carrots adds even more veggies to the recipe. The best part is that your entire meal will be ready when the slow cooker is done, making this a great choice for busy weeknights.

Ingredients:

- 1 lb of turkey, beef or lamb
- 2 cloves of garlic, minced
- ½ cup of water or beef broth
- 2 cups of frozen carrots
- 1 tablespoon of herbs de provence
- 1 onion, chopped
- 2 cups of sweet potatoes, mashed

How to Make It:

Chop the onions, then brown them with the meat in a skillet on medium heat.

Add the minced garlic and the herbs to the pan in the last couple of minutes.

Drain away any fat and place the meat mixture in your slow cooker.

Stir the frozen carrots into the meat mixture, mixing it up to ensure the veggies are well distributed.

Pour the water or beef broth over the meat mixture.

Use a rubber spatula to spread the sweet potatoes on top of the meat mixture.

Cover the slow cooker, allowing to cook for 5-6 hours on low.

30 minutes before eating, change the heat setting to high and remove the lid of the slow cooker. Allow to cook uncovered on high for at least 30 minutes, which makes the mashed sweet potatoes get crispy.

Serve while hot and enjoy the delicious, one-pot casserole.

Servings:

Makes 4 servings.

❧Paleo Pizza Bowl Slow Cooker Casserole❧

You do not have to eat pizza crust to enjoy all the delicious flavors of pizza. This recipe allows you to combine all your favorite pizza ingredients together in a bowl, yet you skip the crust to keep the dish paleo friendly. You will love all the onions, bell peppers and your other favorite toppings. Simply throw this in the slow cooker and enjoy an amazing dinner that comes all in one pot.

Ingredients:

- 2 cups of water
- ½ cup of chopped onion
- ½ cup of chopped bell peppers
- ½ cup of mushrooms, chopped
- 1 tablespoon of olive oil
- ½ teaspoon of honey
- 1 can of tomato paste (12oz)
- 2 teaspoons of oregano
- 2 teaspoons of minced garlic
- 1 teaspoon of basil
- Pepper and salt to taste
- Favorite toppings (ie. tomatoes, ham, paleo friendly sausage, shredded chicken, olives, spinach etc.)

How to Make It:

In a skillet, heat up the olive oil over medium high heat.

Add the minced garlic, onion, bell peppers and mushrooms. Continue to sauté until these ingredients are tender.

Add the water, mixture of sautéed veggies, honey, tomato paste, oregano, basil, pepper and salt to the slow cooker. Mix well until combined.

Cover and turn on low, allowing to cook for 3-4 hours.

About 30 minutes before eating, add your favorite toppings to the slow cooker.

Turn the slow cooker on high and cook partially uncovered, allowing the mixture to become bubbly.

Serve in bowls, topping with paleo friendly cheese if desired. Enjoy!

Servings:

Makes 4 servings.

❧Paleo Eggplant and Buffalo Chicken Lasagna Casserole❧

Once you have the prep time done, all you need to do is turn on the slow cooker and let this dish cook. Dinner will be ready without you needing to cook anything else.

Ingredients:

- 1 purple, large eggplant, thinly sliced
- 2-4 cups of baby spinach, fresh
- 4 cloves of garlic, minced
- 1 medium onion, thinly sliced
- 2 lbs of chicken breasts, boneless and skinless
- 1 cup of paleo friendly hot sauce
- Pepper, parsley and salt to taste

How to Make It:

The night before, use a mandolin slicer to quickly slice up the eggplant, which will help you get uniform slices. Place the eggplant slices in a bowl, covering with water. Allow to soak overnight.

The next day, cut chicken breasts into chunks, pounding with a meat mallet to make chunks very thin. Season with some pepper, parsley and salt.

Drain the eggplant slices and put between paper towels to thoroughly dry them.

Mix together the minced garlic, hot sauce, chicken and onion slices in a big bowl. Stir to make sure the chicken is well coated.

Start layering the casserole in the slow cooker. Add some sauce to the bottom of the slow cooker, top with eggplant slices, add some chicken, top with more sauce, layer in the spinach and then repeat all the layers. Cover the casserole and turn on low, cooking for 5 hours. Serve hot and enjoy.

Servings:

Makes 6-8 servings.

Paleo Sweet Potato and Bacon Slow Cooker Casserole

This delicious recipe takes a little time to put together but it provides a hearty meal. While the eggs may make you think of breakfast, this hash brown casserole makes the perfect dinner, full of protein, fiber and veggies. If you do not mind eating white potatoes, you could always do this recipe with frozen hash browns, but this recipe uses shredded sweet potatoes, since they have less starch in them than regular potatoes do.

Ingredients:

- 6 slices of bacon, uncured
- 1 cup of almond milk
- 1 red bell pepper, chopped
- 12 free range eggs
- 1 teaspoon of dill weed
- 1 medium onion, diced
- 1 clove of garlic, finely minced
- 2 lbs of sweet potatoes, shredded
- Black pepper and salt to taste

How to Make It:

Wash and peel the sweet potatoes, use a grater or a shredding attachment on your food processor to shred the sweet potatoes.

Wash the bell pepper, remove the seeds and chop it into small pieces.

Wash and peel the onion and then dice it.

In a skillet, brown the bacon until crispy. Place on paper towels to drain and cool. Crumble bacon after it cools.

Drain most of the bacon grease, leaving just a bit in the pan.

Add the red bell pepper, garlic and onion to the pan, allowing to cook until it softens.

Add the shredded sweet potatoes and mix together with the onion mixture.

Using coconut oil, grease the inside of your slow cooker to keep the eggs from sticking.

In the prepared slow cooker, add about 1/3 of the sweet potato mixture, topping with 1/3 of the crumbled bacon.

Continue to layer with the rest of the shredded sweet potato mixture and the bacon.

In a large bowl, beat the eggs with the pepper, salt, dill and almond milk. Pour the egg mixture on top of the layers in the slow cooker.

Cover the slow cooker, turning on low and cooking for about 8-10 hours.

Serve while hot and enjoy.

Servings:

Makes 4-6 servings.

❧Paleo Tasty Stuffed Peppers Slow Cooker Casserole❧

This recipe allows you to make an entire meal in your slow cooker, which makes dinner time so easy at the end of a hectic day. The peppers are so good for you and the addition of carrots, onion, garlic and cauliflower makes sure you get even more nutrition from this delicious meal. You will also get plenty of protein from the ground beef or turkey you use for the recipe. Once you make these tasty stuffed peppers, you will definitely want to make this recipe again.

Ingredients:

- ½ head of cauliflower
- 5 ounces of tomato paste
- 1 lb of ground turkey or beef
- 1 large carrot, chopped
- ¼ cup of Italian seasoning
- ¼ cup of beef stock
- 1 medium onion, finely diced
- 4 large bell peppers, any color
- 4 cloves of garlic, finely minced
- Pepper and salt to taste

How to Make It:

Start by placing the carrots, cauliflower, garlic and onion in your food processor, processing until it is very fine.

Remove the tops of the peppers, setting the tops to the side (you need to keep them). Remove all the seeds from the peppers and rinse the peppers out.

In a mixing bowl, mix the meat, seasoning, pepper, salt, tomato paste and veggie mixture. Mix until well combined.

After combining, spoon the meat and veggie mixture into the prepared peppers until they reach the top.

Place the filled peppers in the slow cooker and top with the pepper tops.

Add the beef stock to the bottom of the slow cooker.

Cover the slow cooker, cooking for about 6-8 hours on low.

Serve 1 pepper per person and enjoy hot.

Servings:

Makes 4 servings.

Chapter 8: Paleo Slow Cooker Drink and Dessert Recipes

Yes, even desserts and drinks can be whipped up in your slow cooker and these recipes are all paleo friendly. For a cool night with friends, the cinnamon and orange apple cider is sure to warm everyone up. The stuffed apples make a great dessert anytime and you can put on the spiced pumpkin latte recipe the night before so you have a nice drink to enjoy as you wake up in the morning. When you want a sweet treat while sticking to the paleo diet, these recipes will not disappoint.

❧Cinnamon and Orange Slow Cooker Apple Cider❧

When you want a delicious, naturally sweet drink to warm you up and sooth your sinuses, this cinnamon and orange slow cooker apple cider is the perfect choice. The honey adds a hint of sweetness, while the cinnamon and cloves adds a spiciness that tempts your taste buds. The addition of the orange juice and rind adds a citrus twist to the cider, making a tasty drink that you will want to make again and again.

Ingredients:

- ½ teaspoon of whole cloves (organic if possible)
- 8 cups of apple cider
- Juice and rind of one orange
- 1 tablespoon of raw honey, organic
- 2 cinnamon sticks, organic

How to Make It:

Place the apple cider in the slow cooker.

Juice the orange, adding the juice into the apple cider.

Cut the orange rind into pieces, adding them to the slow cooker.

Place the honey, cloves and cinnamon sticks in the slow cooker. Stir the contents to combine thoroughly.

Cover and turn the slow cooker on high, allowing to cook for about 3 hours.

Turn on warm to keep warm until you are ready to drink the apple cider.

Enjoy with an extra cinnamon stick if desired.

Servings:

Makes 8 servings.

❧Paleo Spiced Pumpkin Latte Slow Cooker Recipe❧

Instead of heading to a local coffee shop for a latte that does not fit into your paleo diet, you can make your own paleo latte that smells and tastes amazing. The pumpkin adds delicious flavor and the coconut milk gives you the latte texture and flavor without the dairy. Agave nectar adds sweetness and the nutmeg, cinnamon and cloves spice up the latte.

Ingredients:

- 1 cup of brewed coffee of choice
- 2 teaspoons of vanilla
- 1/8 teaspoon of nutmeg
- 1 can of coconut milk (14oz)
- Dash of ginger
- 3 tablespoons of canned pumpkin
- ¼ teaspoon of cinnamon
- 1 tablespoon of agave nectar
- 1/8 teaspoon of cloves

How to Make It:

Place all the ingredients in the slow cooker. Stir together to combine thoroughly.

Turn on low and allow to cook for 2-3 hours.

Serve hot. Add a little honey if desired for extra sweetness.

Servings:

Makes 2-3 servings.

Paleo Apple and Pear Sauce Slow Cooker Recipe

This apple and pear sauce makes a delicious treat when you are craving something sweet. While you could serve it as a side dish when fixing a pork dinner, it makes a wonderful dessert. You can eat it warm, or you can refrigerate it and enjoy it cold as well. For a more complicated flavor, add several different types of pears and apples to the recipe instead of only using one type of pear and apple.

Ingredients:

- 1 pound of pears (choose several different types)
- 4 pounds of apples (choose several different types)
- 1 navel orange, juiced
- 1 tablespoon of cinnamon
- ¼ cup of honey, raw
- 1/8 cup of water

How to Make It:

Peel and core the pears and apples and then cut them into large chunks.

Place all the ingredients in the slow cooker. Cover and turn on low.

Cook for 2 hours, stirring every 20-30 minutes and using a spoon to break down the fruit.

Cook for 6-8 more hours, or overnight.

When the apple pear sauce is complete, use a spoon to stir and break up the fruit for chunky sauce. For a smoother sauce, blend with an immersion blender.

Serve warm or allow to cool and serve cold.

Any leftovers should be refrigerated in an airtight container for up to 5 days.

Servings:

Makes 6-10 servings, depending on serving size.

❧Paleo Stuffed Apple Slow Cooker Recipe❧

For a sweet treat, these apples make the perfect dessert. The natural sugar from the green apples provides plenty of sweetness and the shredded coconut really adds flavor to this dish. Put this dessert in the crock pot when you come home from work and enjoy it later in the evening. It is easy to make and it only takes about 10 minutes of prep time.

Ingredients:

- ½ cup of homemade coconut butter (or you can use coconut cream concentrate)
- 3-4 tablespoons of shredded coconut, unsweetened
- ¼ cup of nut butter of choice
- 1 cup of water
- Pinch of salt
- ¼ teaspoon of nutmeg
- 2-3 tablespoons of cinnamon
- 4 medium green apples, cores removed

How to Make It:

Start by using an apple corer to core the apples to make it easy. Make sure that you leave the bottom of the apple intact as much as possible.

In a bowl, mix the nut butter, nutmeg, cinnamon, salt and coconut butter. Mix well until totally combined.

Set the apples in the slow cooker, pouring the water into the bottom of the slow cooker.

Using a spoon, stuff the middle of the apples with the coconut butter mixture. After stuffing, add shredded coconut to the top and sprinkle with a little more cinnamon to taste.

Cover and turn on low, allowing to cook for about 2-3 hours. The apples become softer the longer you cook them, so test for softness and choose your desired level of softness.

Serve the apples while warm, sprinkling with a bit more coconut if desired.

Enjoy.

Servings:

Makes 4 servings.

&Paleo Poached Honeyed Pears Slow Cooker Recipe&

Honeyed pears are soothing and sweet. They make for a relaxing dessert and they are wonderful for the stomach as well. This recipe makes 8 servings, which makes it perfect for serving up dinner guests. You can always save the extras for a healthy, sweet snack later if you actually end up with any leftovers.

Ingredients:

- 4 tablespoons of arrowroot powder
- 1 1/3 cup of honey, raw
- 4 tablespoons of orange juice
- 1/8 teaspoon of nutmeg
- 2 tablespoons of water
- ¼ teaspoon of ginger, ground
- ½ teaspoon of cinnamon
- 8 pears (any pears of choice)

How to Make It:

Working from the bottom of the pears, remove the core, allowing the pear stems to stay intact. Leave the skins on the pears. After coring, place the pears in the slow cooker.

In a small bowl, mix the ginger, water, honey, nutmeg and cinnamon.

Mix well and then pour the honey mixture on top of the pears.

Cover the pears, cooking for 2-3 hours on high. Once pears are tender (don't let them get mushy), they are done.

Take pears out of the slow cooker, setting to the side.

Add the orange juice and arrowroot powder to the juices in the slow cooker, stirring well to combine.

Allow the liquid to cook on high for 10-15 more minutes until the sauce begins to thicken.

Place pears in shallow bowls.

Spoon the honey liquid over the pears and serve while warm.

Enjoy the sweet, honeyed pears.

Servings:

Makes 8 servings.

❧Paleo Bananas Foster Slow Cooker Recipe❧

While this dessert is a bit high in natural sugar, it is totally delicious. Save it for an occasional treat or whip up this tasty dish for guests. The lemon juice, cloves, nutmeg, cinnamon, honey and coconut oil all combine with the bananas for a sweet, tasty flavor that is sure to satisfy any craving for something sweet. While it tastes wonderful warm, you will enjoy any leftovers just as well when they are cold, so keep those leftovers if you actually have any. The recipe only makes 4 servings, but you can easily double it if you want to serve more people or you want to have leftovers for a late night snack.

Ingredients:

-   1 heaping tablespoon of coconut oil
-   3 tablespoons of honey
-   ¼ teaspoon of cinnamon
-   1/8 teaspoon of nutmeg
-   1 tablespoon of lemon juice
-   Pinch of cloves
-   4 medium bananas, medium firm

How to Make It:

Place all the ingredients except for the bananas in your slow cooker.

Turn the slow cooker to high and allow the coconut oil to melt.

Once the ingredients melt, stir together well until thoroughly combined.

Turn the heat on the slow cooker to low.

Slice bananas into slices about ¼ inch thick. Place the sliced bananas in the slow cooker.

Carefully toss the bananas with the honey mixture, being careful not to break the banana slices.

Allow to cook for 1.5-2 hours on low.

When bananas are done, divide into four servings. Place each serving on an individual plate.

Spoon some of the honey mixture over the bananas.

Enjoy while warm. Store any leftovers in the refrigerator.

Servings:

Makes 4 servings.

Free Paleo Book

As a thank you for purchasing this book, I am going to give away "The Paleo Green Smoothie" to you absolutely free.

This fantastic book contains 48 paleo friendly recipes such as:

- Sweet Strawberry Mango Spinach Smoothie
- Fruity Coconut Water and Kale
- Kale Almond Butter and Banana

To download your free book, head over to:

http://marthadrummond.com/paleo-slow-cooker-cookbook-bonus/

I hope you enjoy them. I will likely be publishing this book soon and when I do this offer will be taken down, so get your free book while you still can.

Martha

Other Cookbooks by Martha Drummond

The Vegan Slow Cooker Cookbook

The Paleo Comfort Foods Cookbook

The Breakfast Sandwich Maker Cookbook

The Ketogenic Cookbook